ADDITIONAL PRAISE FOR *The Weight of Desire*

Jina Carvalho's poetry is gripping and filled with vignettes that are moving, poignant and original. The sweep of topics range from motherhood to violation, to disorienting technology and most viscerally, to marriage, bodies and lovers. An impressive debut collection.

—Dr. Elaine Gale, Writing Center Director
Antioch University Graduate School for Leadership and Change

These are poems of passion in all its manifestations—sanctioned and forbidden, unrequited and reciprocal. In *The Weight of Desire*, Jina Carvalho reveals her secrets, many of which you will be unable to forget.

—David Starkey, Santa Barbara Poet Laureate (2009-2011)
Author of *Like a Soprano*

© 2019 Jina Carvalho
www.JinaCarvalho.com

Published by Sungold Editions
Book Design by Chryss Yost
www.sungoldeditions.com

Author Phto: Alexa Hope Rakow
Cover Photo: Annie Spratt, "Wall in the Alfama, Lisbon Portugal"

ISBN-13: 978-0-9991678-2-3

The Weight of Desire:
A Poetry Memoir

Poems by

Jina Carvalho

Sungold Editions • Santa Barbara
2019

This book is for Wally

Contents

The Immigrant	11
Cracked Screen	13
She Sneaks in a Poem	14
I Once Lived in a House like Hers	15
Son	16
Questions for Mothers of Sons	17
This Month I Started Collecting the Blood	18
Spider Grandmother	21
Sparkling Lucy in the Sky	22
The Immigrant: Part 2	23
Desire in the Immigrant World	24
Paranoia	25
Man Carving Totem Pole	26
R.D Laing	27
Secrets: Part 1	29
Secrets: Part 2	31
Tumble Free	36
Surfer at the Laundromat	37
The Hunger	38
Love Etched Our Faces	39
Hey Want to Get Married?	40
Malibu Night Drive	41
Edwin's Shneidman's Death	42
One moment	44
Friendship of Women	45
Holding Hands	46
Healing	47
The Immigrant: Part 3	48

For my friends who stood by me through the anxiety, fear and endless rewrites. Joyce Catlett, Lena Firestone, Diana Raab, Maureen Sullivan, Katherine Morrow, Laure-Anne Bosselaar, Sherise Prince.

Deryl, who for so long, has encouraged me to express myself.

Bob, whose courage to live an authentic life inspired me to live mine and to write this book.

Marlon, when I became a mother, I felt such joy and knew I wanted you to have a different life. I made a commitment to face difficult truths about myself and my past, many of which I share in this collection of poems.

In memory of my dear friends Anne Baker, Fred Branfman, Zsuzsua Beres and Barry Langberg.

Finally, to my wonderful and patient editors Perie Longo and publisher Chryss Yost.

Triumphantly, with arms raised high, I shout "Hooray, it's out in the world, at last."

The Immigrant

The first day of school in Elliott Lake, Canada
I sit quietly hands folded on my wooden desk
listening to words
I don't understand
I try hard
I am the new girl in the class
from another country
I watch what the girl next to me is doing
I copy
I try hard
I look around
the bell rings
we go outside
it's recess
I follow
alone
I smile
try hard
to play
I am wearing a handmade dress
gray woolen jumper with red pleats
carefully stitched and pressed
I look at the other girls clothes
they are not like mine
I look down
I hate my dress
the other girls
blond fair and tall
my small dark self shrinks

into the back of the playground
I try hard
on this first day of school
watch wait imitate
never ask
pretend I understand
sit quietly
hands folded on the wooden desk
and smile

Cracked Screen

I ran over my computer
when I backed up my car
now I write on a distorted surface
cracked screen
edges bleed into the center
shattered glass forms jagged lines
black swirling border
plants itself
on the top right corner of the screen
I begin…

She Sneaks in a Poem

Parking next to a freeway onramp
in the morning rush hour
she sneaks in a poem

looking up
she recognizes
her own face
in the rear view mirror

softly she opens her hand
placing it on her smiling face
she sneaks in another poem

I Once Lived in a House like Hers

I had a baby
toilet seat protectors
shiny hardwood floors
a husband
well-tended yard
fruit trees and rose bushes
mornings filled with tender hugs
from tiny outstretched arms
fragrant bouquet of flesh
against my breast

in that quiet little house
my eyes grew downcast
careful not to show
how trapped I felt
living
in a house like hers

Son

for Marlon

I search for his tiny outline

against a blinding afternoon sun

with waves tumbling him

joyously in from the sea

his shape

the curve of his body

so familiar

waves spitting him

laughing

at my feet

Questions for Mothers of Sons

Do you play mother
dressed in duty and obligation?

Do you warn him
never to betray you
binding him in filial love?

Are you training him
to fall in rank and file
mother to son?

Who were you
before you were a mother?
where have you hidden her?

He is searching everywhere
for her
a hidden key lies
buried beneath your pillow
in the bed
you now sleep in
alone

This Month I Started Collecting the Blood

Bright, red, clean
it flows month after month
year after year
centuries of secrecy and shame
flushed, buried, hidden
a wound that will not heal
a nagging
an enemy

This month I started collecting the blood

what do I do with it?
not something you ask a lot of questions about
secret glances at the drugstore checkout
boxes quietly stuffed into brown paper bags
every month the cold silent wait
then it comes
out of hiding
sheds runs, repeats

This month I started collecting the blood

blood
a sign of danger
life slipping away
precious red liquid
contained at any cost
"The gift of Life"
pouring out of me

what people die for
flushed away
unpure
unwanted
not from the vein
but from the wound between my legs
how many gallons does a woman spill in a lifetime?
is there more bloodshed by every woman
every month and with every birth
than men could rival in war
our bleeding will never stop
if a woman's blood
is not allowed to flow with dignity
then shall it flow in the streets

This month I wondered if the bleeding would ever start
Now I wonder if it will ever stop
I remember my mother
bleeding for weeks
afraid to see a doctor
knowing something was wrong
a young woman
secretly knowing something was desperately wrong

when my son was born
I did not see the blood
he was cut out
neat and clean
he was wiped
and I was stitched

I asked the doctor to sneak out my placenta

not thrown in some garbage bin
he carefully wrapped it
labeled it
put it in the freezer
at the nurses station
after three days
a revolted nurse
wanted the well wrapped placenta
out of the freezer

no room for the blood
I checked out of that establishment
baby and placenta in hand
not clear about what to do with either

that night under a full moon
I dug a hole
I placed the placenta in it
and buried it
under our only birch tree in the yard
ending in the only way I knew
our mystery of blood

Spider Grandmother

for my Portuguese grandmother Amilia Rei

I was born in my mother's mother's house
on a cornhusk bed
she was our midwife
gently bathing us
spinning memory webs
deep into my body
around my heart

I will clear a large wall for her
draw a giant web
for this gypsy grandmother
black and veiled
talking in tongues
channeling voices of the dead
capturing me
under her spell

Sparkling Lucy in the Sky

for my granddaughter Lucy Talia

Wide open gaze
reminds me of your father
at our moment of recognition
that baby boy
who stared me down
now your father
staring back at you
Lucy, your light shines
illuminating our beauty and splendor
our memories and shadows

The Immigrant: Part 2

Who are you to judge me
from your academic high rise
filled with fancy words and prizes
you gaze down
with perfect form
calm cool and in control
you know nothing about me
I try hard for your approval
I hate the power
I have given you

Desire in the Immigrant World

Buy a book
don't dive in
put it aside
sneak in the pleasure
in dribs and drabs

in a hot crowded restaurant
I sit alone at a large table
in the cool shade
scanning around
guiltily
I move
to a smaller table
in the hot sun

Paranoia

They're looking at you
don't let it show
keep quiet
you look strange
you're too quiet now
say something
don't draw attention to yourself
say something
say it this way
no
that way
no
like this
they will know you are OK
if you say that
just like that

Man Carving Totem Pole

In the alley

along the railway track

among abandoned cars and concrete

ancestors not forgotten

man
                      carving

totem pole

R.D Laing

for Ronnie

I first saw you winter of '73
snow on streets of a Montreal night
Hare Krishnas chanting
you meditated on the stage
of the great cathedral
enchanting me
with your stuttering Scottish brogue
spinning hypnotic yarns from your trip to the East
medical students lined the aisles
to the microphones
hounding the "eminent psychiatrist"
to answer questions about schizophrenia
you refused
sharing instead fragments of eastern thought
"you make no sense" they shouted
accusing you of madness
the label stuck
you were a legend in '73
I was running from home
crazy lost afraid
that night
I was calm
without knowing why
what did you teach?
it might be possible
you never taught anything
you were just a man
who lived and died

a man who looked upon the sorrows of the world
with great compassion
and questioned

Secrets: Part 1

I

The young girl enters a basement bedroom.
She is very slight for her 6 years, her large brown eyes welcoming to the man who gestures her in.
He closes the door softly behind them, sits on the edge of the double bed and swoops her onto his lap. She giggles and puts her arms around his neck.
She loves the man who lives in-the basement of her parent's house; he is the only one always ready to play with her.

II

Her favorite game is the tickling game.
He lies on the bed and she lies on top of him. He tickles her everywhere and she tickles him, everywhere.
Then exhausted and sweaty they play "horsey"; she straddles his waist like she's riding a horse. She sits on the saddle which is always a hard thing under her, when she rubs against it, it always feels so good.
He asks her to ride and ride and gallop faster and faster. Until the "horse" is too wet and exhausted to go any further.
The saddle feels good to her, makes her body tickle and get hot between her legs.
She loves the game so much and would play anytime she could.

III

One day
The man's wife came in when they were playing horsey.
She got very, very mad.
She scared the little girl and told her she was a bad dirty girl and told her to get out.
The girl ran out, she cried and cried outside the man's room.
She could hear the woman yelling at her husband, calling him names.
The girl knew she had been very bad and it was her fault.
She would never play that game again

IV

The man warned her never to tell
What they had done was bad and she would get in trouble.
Never, never, never tell.
She promised.
It was on that day her large brown eyes filled with tears and fear.
She said good bye to the man.
She never played with him again.

Secrets: Part 2

I

At 16, she never thought of herself as pretty, but she wanted to look pretty.
She sewed herself a flowing, long dress, in the hippy style of the 60's. It had a dark brown background with white daisies and lace around the neck.
She loved the dress.

She was going to wear it to the weekend pop festival, an outdoor happening with bands, lots of pot, food and dancing. The festival was thrilling. The music flowed on for days, and she danced and partied.
She was so happy to be alive.

She noticed on the next blanket, a boy her age with a guitar. He had the most beautiful smile and smiled a lot at her. It made her feel so good inside to look at him and have him look back at her in that way. He had curly light brown hair that fell to his shoulders; he had such a chiseled beautiful face. She couldn't get enough of looking at him.

He looked at her in that way. At her! She couldn't believe it, when at the end of the day, he asked her to sit on the hillside beside him. He sang and played his guitar for her. He sang love songs. She had never felt like this before.
She wondered if this was love.

Then he kissed her. He told her that he liked her and kept kissing

her and she kissed him back. She did not know if she was kissing him "good". She just wanted to kiss and kiss forever and press her body into his. It melted in the heat she felt inside.
She was a soft open mass, unable to stop.
Not wanting to stop.

II

He asked for her phone number. She couldn't believe he liked her. Maybe he liked her the way she liked him. They kissed more. They kissed until it was too late to sit on the dark hill anymore. She knew she would get in trouble with her parents. She was not allowed out with boys. They were old fashioned Portuguese. She was not supposed to be doing this until she was married.
She was a bad girl.

But it felt so good, and he liked her.. and maybe he would marry her.. maybe he was the one.. he must be, because of how she felt ... She knew she loved him.

III

He did call her.
They met at places where they could kiss and hold each other and get excited. It was their secret. It felt wrong and right at the same time. She wanted him to touch her everywhere because of how nice it felt. She knew it was wrong. But she did it anyway.

She would just not tell.
No one needed to know. She loved him and she would do anything for him. He must love her because he wanted her to touch him.
He must love her.

IV

She made a decision.
She would let him make love to her. Go all the way. He wanted it and she wanted him. No one needed to know. She was old enough and she knew lots of girls who had done it. She loved him and he loved her.
He told her he loved her when they were kissing and holding each other. He told her he wanted her, he wanted to make love to her. He asked her to get pills, so they wouldn't get in trouble.
She knew where to get them and she decided to go there. She got them. She made up her mind.
She wanted to do it.

V

She made love to him.
She cried when they finished because she let him inside her. It hurt, but that is not why she cried. She cried because she was a woman now. There was no turning back. Now she had a big secret from her mother. She could never tell.
She was a bad girl.

They made love in his room in his parents' house. He lived in beautiful house in the richest part of town. He had a maid and butler. She had never been in a house like that.
She felt so out of place. She knew they did not approve of her. She was not good enough for him. But he loved her.
She couldn't believe he loved her.

VI

He stopped calling her.
She waited everyday he never called. She cried every night.
He didn't call her.
One day he asked her to come over to his house. When he opened the door
He did not kiss her.

VII

He was cold.
She was terrified.
She was so afraid of what was happening. He asked her to sit down. He picked up his guitar and played her song. She was too afraid to cry. He told her he couldn't see her anymore. This was the last time. It was goodbye.
"But you said you loved me?" she cried.
"I don't love you now. I don't think I ever loved you. You're a nice girl, but I don't love you anymore.
So, we can't go out anymore".

VIII

She remembered getting up and walking out the door.
She was numb. She walked into the cold snowy Toronto night. She walked and walked all the way home. It must have been several miles. She couldn't remember how she got home.
She cried most of the way. And thought she would kill herself.
She was so ashamed to be rejected like that. She could only die to end the pain inside.
There was no other way out.

IX

How could she trust anyone again?
She was wrong about him. How could she ever know again if she was right? NO, he had to love her. His parents must have turned him against her. That's what happened. She was sure of it. But he told her he did not love her, why did he say that? He said he never loved her.
How could he say that?

X

She began to pretend it never happened. The secret never happened, she must nor tell anyone especially her mother. Never tell that he said he never loved her. She couldn't tell anyone. She would never do that with anyone.
Ever

Tumble Free

Under the weight of desire
turn and kiss the lips
nearest to you
do not shut your eyes

let the sweetness run down your legs
in the orange afternoon light
rush against the door
hurl it shut
push against the force
that can take you away
from this moment

Surfer at the Laundromat

Oh the way, he uncorked my bottle
that Saturday afternoon
at the laundromat
I would have eagerly followed him
into the surf
I was restless
he was so young and fresh
my hands
slowly continued
to fold the laundry
but my eyes
fell elsewhere

The Hunger

She waits
arranging herself
for him

the door opens slowly
she holds back
her excitement

his indifference excites her
she wants to pull him to her
make love to him
over and over
until he fills the hunger
she knows
only he
can satisfy

Love Etched Our Faces

for Wally

In the fading afternoon light
I sit on our bed
reading maps
planning our next adventure
new vistas
tender nights
lazy mornings
exploring territories
of the heart
meandering open roads
music pulsing
life rushing ahead
too quickly
our youth tucked safely inside
love etching our faces
lines on a roadmap
of our life together
hearts tattooed
by a quarter century
of passion and surrender
with the good fortune
of finding each other

Hey Want to Get Married?

for Wally, my third husband

Why?
I answer quickly
married again?
pause
I look at you
ask again
hey, want to get married?
my heart now beating
slowly
tenderly
opening to you
I take a deep breath
sure, I say
sure

Malibu Night Drive

Half way home
exhausted
even the sun drops to the ground
at my feet
it cries out
take me
carry me
pass me on to the moonlight
I need rest
my arm outstretched
I slowly walk
into the night
to capture
the remaining light
in my open palm
and continue my journey home

Edwin's Shneidman's Death

for Ed

Good enough death
for the old man
father of suicidology

our friendship
like a rope
plaited strands of joy and anger
now gone slack
we cannot make water flow back
return fire to flint

not being a serious student
I disappointed you
like many others
robbing you of your legacy

Psychache you named the despairing soul
shaping our world with language
essential Shneidman
feared father
benevolent friend
you leave a void

I write no essay
only lazy fragments
now sinking
in Melville's sea

cutout paper doll you made me
smiles on my desk
slyly reminding me
"My beauty" you called me
"my good man" I called you
 were you lonely?

One moment

> *for Ken, who died raking his lawn*

You'll close your eyes
one time too many times
one moment
one insignificant moment
when you open a door
ride a city bus
walk your dog
rake your lawn
a simple moment
while you arrange your closet
eat your cereal
play your piano
nothing will be spoken
the sky will not open
lightning will not strike
nothing will mark the moment
when it all passes on
without you

Friendship of Women

I no longer need your approval
and share my life with you
I no longer need you to scold me
and hear your concerns
I no longer need you to be angry
and hear your disappointment
I no longer need your rejection
and tell you what I think
I no longer need your praise
and feel my own confidence
I no longer need you to save me
and can be alone
I no longer need you to be my mother
and know things for myself
I no longer need you to approve of me
and can accept your feelings for me
I no longer need to put you above me
and accept your friendship

Holding Hands

On Sunday night
I sat beside you
you held my hand
a simple action
reminding me
of so many moments
over years
of our deep friendship

Healing

for Maureen Carruthers

Love laid me under her great cape
caressing the dark pain in my back
hard tight flesh
had turned to stone
"do not be afraid"
love whispered
as she nestled me
to her great chest

Love ruptured through the darkness
bringing me wise figures
visions and songs
to dance around my bed
love fed me rivers and trees
love was not delicate
love was fierce in her desire
to do what was necessary
for the healing

When the surgeons arrived
to remove the darkened stone
from my back
they found nothing

The Immigrant: Part 3

From the illiterate immigrant house
plastic covered couches
crucifix covered walls
glow in the dark
our Lady of Fatima statues
I emerge
fleshy and female
I ascend
from under
the weight of desire

www.ingramcontent.com/pod-product-compliance
Lightning Source LLC
Chambersburg PA
CBHW030459010526
44118CB00011B/1007